THE WORST CLASS IN THE SCHOOL

COLIN FLETCHER

Illustrations by
STEWART CURRY

POOLBEG
FOR CHILDREN

Published 1999 by
Poolbeg Press Ltd
123 Baldoyle Industrial Estate
Dublin 13, Ireland

Text © Colin Fletcher 1999
Illustrations © Stewart Curry 1999

The moral right of the author has been asserted.

The Arts Council
An Chomhairle Ealaíon

A catalogue record for this book is available from the British Library.

ISBN 1 85371 936 6

Illustrations by Stewart Curry
Cover design by Artmark
Set by Poolbeg Group Services Ltd in Times 15/24
Printed by The Guernsey Press Ltd,
Vale, Guernsey, Channel Islands.

To all those who have been in
1F, 2F, 4F, or 5F

Amazing Amelia

"Hey, everybody! Look!
Watch this for a trick!
My eyes roll in my head
Till they're white like when you're dead.
I'm looking at my brains –
They're all purple worms and veins.
My little brother, Jude,
Wet himself and pooed!

Hey! Get this! Look at me!
I'm double-jointed, see?
My fingers pull right back.
You can hear the knuckles crack.
I can twist my knee right round
And bend back and lick the ground.
My little sister, Vic,
Turned yellow and was sick!

Hey, you lot! Over here!

Watch my stomach disappear!

I force myself right in

Till I'm mega-mega-thin.

I just hold my breath. It's smart!

That's my spine and that's my heart."

"Oh Miss, Amelia Head

Has fainted OR IS DEAD!"

Bossy Bessy

"Off my table!
Off my chair!
Get my folder!
Put it there!"

Bossy Bessy
Scares us dead,
Frightens Miss
And bullies the Head.

"Let's play rounders!
I'm in bat!
No ball, Ian!
I'm not out!"

Bossy Bessy
Pokes and punches,
Takes our things
And eats our lunches.

"I'M with Sally!
YOU go away!
She's MY friend
Because I say!"

Bossy Bessy
Swears and lies,
NEVER gives in
And NEVER cries.

"Stop that, Bessy!
I'll smack your bum!
Bend down, Bessy!"
THAT'S HER MUM!

Creepy Chrissy

"I like your hair-do, Miss.

It makes you look so young.

I adore the maths you do with us –

You make it all such fun."

Creep! Creep! Creep!

Lick! Lick! Lick!

Fingers down your throat! She makes you sick!

"Thank you for the housepoint, Miss.

I don't deserve it really.

Please give one to little Jack.

He spoke up then, so clearly."

Suck! Suck! Suck!

Crawl! Crawl! Crawl!

She never does anything wrong at all.

Till yesterday in geography,

When Tara went and told

That Chrissy was writing SWEAR-WORDS

Behind her map of the world!

Miss said: "Chrissy, come here child."

And Chrissy! Well! SHE JUST WENT WILD!

"I hate you Tara!" Chrissy yelled.

"You sneak! You tell-tale tart!"

She bawled! She scrabbed! She swore as well!

She ripped her map apart!

I liked her, then, all fierce and mad.

Yeah, underneath, she's not so bad.

Dangerous Danny

Danny makes your fingers crack
And jerks your arm behind behind your back.

      "No, Danny! No!
      Please! My arm won't bend!
      Yeow, Danny! Yeow!
      You know that I'm your friend!"

Danny grabs your nose and turns
And twists your wrists with Chinese burns.

      "No more, Danny! No more!
      I lied! I haven't seen ye!
      Cor, Danny! Cor!
      You didn't snog with Xenia!"

Danny grabs and Danny jabs you,
Gets his pencil sharp and stabs you.

> "Ouch, Danny! Ouch!
> Stop! You really hurt!
> Yeowch, Danny! Yeowch!
> You're ruining my shirt!"

Danny whips your legs with sticks,
Pulls your ear out hard and flicks.

> "Ah, Danny! Ah!
> My eye's got something in it!
> Yah, Danny! Yah!
> My mum's coming in a minute!"

"DANNY'S FACE IS CUT FROM STONE!
HIS HEAD IS HARD. IT'S SOLID BONE!"

"Oof, Danny! Oof!
I didn't mean that, really!
Get off, Danny! Get off!
I broke that arm once, nearly!"

Exploding Ed

"Hey! Look at Ed!
He's round as a moon!
All swollen and red
Like a massive balloon!

Take cover! Get out!
Evacuate the road!
Gas alert! Gas alert!
Ed's gonna explode!"

"I've had coke and a fruitcake,
Some beans and Milk Tray.
Now here comes a bum-quake
They'll hear in Bombay."

"Oh, Ed! What a show-off!
What a BOOM! What a CRUMP!
A world record blow-off!
A ten-kilotonne trump!

We're leaving, Miss Quilter!
Come on, everyone!
Down the Ed-raid shelter!
Put your gas-masks on!"

"Oh, don't go and leave us!
I'm famous. Well-known!
Oh, why are we superstars
Always alone?"

Flashy Floyd

"Our car's a BMW!
Three-litre! Automatic!
Our house has got SIX bedrooms!
YOURS would go in our attic!

This jacket came from Harrods.
Highland leather. Guaranteed.
YOURS was from 'World of Plastic'!
Imitation PVC!

I've got a TV in my pocket.
It cost five hundred quid!
It's got Sky TV and cable!
I mustn't show other kids.

My bike's got real suspension
And THIRTY-SEVEN GEARS!
And my goalie-top is latexed –
Like the England goalie wears.

My dad got this watch in Dallas.
You can wear it undersea!
YOURS looks like a toy one.
It probably cost 3p!"

"Coo, Floyd! Your parents are loaded!
They buy the best! The tops!
But YOU were on special offer
From one of those reject shops!"

Graffiti Greg

'Rosie Nightingale
Kisses like a whale'
Is scrawled in shiny red
On the caretaker's shed.

'Martin McNair
Irons his hair'
Is carved on a tree
Where everyone can see.

'Save the planet!
Throw off Edward Stannett!'
Is felt-tipped on the wall
In the main school hall.

'Ursula thinks she's posh
But she smells and doesn't wash!'
It says on her chair,
On her desk and everywhere.

'Paul woz 'ere!
ONCE this year!'
Is sprayed across the gate
Where all the mothers wait.

'Bessy rules, okay?
No way! No way!'
It says in tiny writing
On the switch for 'Outside Lighting'.

Suddenly, at Valentine's,
A brand new sign appeared.
The paint was Jack's, the spray was mine,

The messsage we all shared.
It was huge and caretaker-proof,
High up on the infants' roof:

'GREG LOVES BESSY,
BESSY LOVES ED,
ED LOVES CHRISSIE,
CHRISSIE LOVES JED,
JED LOVES ANN,
ANN LOVES CLEGG,
CLEGG LOVES NO-ONE
AND NO-ONE LOVES GREG!'

Hurricane Harry

"Mum! Myschoolbag'sreallyinastate!

There'sjustonerottentrainer! WHATASMELL!

Here'sDanny'sfootballshirt. It'snumbereight.

AndWillyParker'sunderpantsaswell!"

"Harry!

I give up!

You're just a hopeless case!

You hurry, hurtle and hop!

You rip, roar and race!

It's Sports Day after lunch.

And I'll be there. Alright?

So sit still on the bench,

Out of everybody's sight!"

"Hasanybodyseenmychocolatebar?

Youplayingfooty? Letmehavetheball!

Ohno! Ican'trememberwhereweare

Whenplaytime'sover. Areweinthehall?"

"Harry!

Mess off!

You're always in the way!

You barge, bump and biff!

You fling, flip and flay!

It's Sports this afternoon.

Parents will be there.

You stay sitting down.

Just watch. Don't interfere!"

"MissI'vedonemywork! I'mfirstagain!

I'vewrittenmasses! Lotsandlotsandlots!

It'sinfelttip. Icouldn'tfindmypen.

It'scalled,justlikeyousaid,'MyFavritSpots'."

18

"Harry!

What drivel!

How dare you say you've done?

You scurry, scrawl and scribble!

You rev, rush and run!

It's 'Sports', not 'Spots', you dope!

Oh really! What a mess!

After lunch, I hope

You don't spoil it for the rest!"

"OhMrLewishaveyouseenmyclass?

Ididn'thearwhatMisssaid. Where'vetheygone?

Shouldweallbesittingonthegrass?

OrshouldIgoandputmygameskiton?"

"Harry!

You don't listen!

You shouldn't be at the start!

19

You hurry, hurtle and hasten!

You dip, dash and dart!

Well, now you're here, you jolly well can do it!

One thousand metres! Just the thing for you!

AND NOW, TODAY'S BIG RACE!

OH, CHEER THEM THROUGH IT!

ARE YOU READY? ARE YOU STEADY?

GO!"

"Harry'sinthelead! He'srunninglikeahero!

He'slefttherestbehind! Justwatchhimrun!

Ican'tbelievehistime! Twotenpointzero!

Thefinallap! Theboycan'tstop! HE'SWON!

Harry!

You're great!

The school's fastest boy!

You speed, sprint and spurt!

You flash, fleet and fly!

JUSTGIVEAHANDTOHARRY!

OURGREATESTRUNNER!

WHATLEGSHEHAS! WHATCOURAGE!

ANDWHATSTYLE!

HE'SBOUNDTOBEANOLYMPICMEDAL

WINNER!

OH,HARRY!

WE'REPROUDTOHAVEYOUINTHESCHOOL!"

Insulting Ian

"Frog face!

Bogey nose!

Monkey brain!

TWIT!

Gas bum!

Sausage toes!

Radar ears!

NIT!"

That's Ian being rude,

When he's in a bad mood.

"Jelly Belly!

Crater mouth!

Flipper feet!

JERK!

Hedgehog hair!
Garlic breath!
Dracula teeth!
BERK!"

That's Ian McBright,
When he's being polite!

J-Jumpy J-Jack

D-D-D-D-Don't!

P-P-P-P-Please!

Balloons m-make me jump!

Kn-knock my kn-kn-knees.

B-Bangs and cr-cr-crashes

M-Make my tummy quake.

S-Sudden sm-sm-smashes

M-Make me sh-sh-shake.

D-Doors sl-sl-sl-slamming

M-Make me go all quivery,

C-Cold and cl-cl-clammy

And sh-sh-sh-sh-shivery.

I never put the light out.

I sleep with Dad and Mum

And sixteen little teddies

And my th-th-th-th-thumb.

I'm scared of n-n-noises.

"H-Help! H-Help!" I yell.

I'm frightened of b-boyses

And g-g-girls as well.

P-P-P-P-Please!

D-D-D-D-Don't

P-Pop those b-balloons.

S-Say, s-say you won't!

B-BANG!

    Oh, where's the l-l . . . ?

B-BANG!

    Oh, where's the l . . . ?

B-BANG!

    I need the l-l . . . !

TOO LATE!

    I'VE WET MY P . . . !

Ketchup Kelly

Please pass the sauce.

Just for the starter course.

This salad is grotesque!

It's like chewing bits of desk!

A dolloping of 'Brown'
Will help the lettuce down.

Please pass the sauce.

Just for this main course.

Salmon quiche is really ghastly!

It tastes of poo and stinks of parsley!

Some squidgy 'Tomato Paste'
Will take away the taste.

Please pass the sauce.

Just for the afters course.

Yuk! Apple pie and custard!

I'm splodging on some mustard!

And pass the 'Hot and Spicy', Bess.

I'm making custard curry! Yes!

Please pass the sauces.

Just for the sauces courses.

'Soy,' 'Horse-raddish,' 'Worcestershire,'

And squirt some 'Daddies' on, just here.

Now . . . . mix it up and fry it

For a healthy, balanced diet!

Lipstick Lizzie

It just ain't fair! Nothin's fair!

It isn't fair! It's not!

They don't care if I'm not there!

An' I don't care! So what!

"Now dress up smart!" Old Quilter moaned.

"And freshen up your face.

The School Inspector's coming round!"

So I dolled up REAL ACE!

My lovely lipstick, 'Midnight Rose',

Pushed on hard and thick.

All red an' sexy. Loads an' loads.

Almost half the stick!

My Totty-Teeny mini-skirt.
A dingly-dangly star.
Platform shoes. A low-cut shirt.
My sister's wonder-bra.
An' when I got to school
The others clapped an' cheered.
"Oh Miss! Don't she look cool!"
But Miss looked white and weird.

"Oh, what have you done?" she spluttered.
"It took me an hour!" I yelled.
"Oh, where are my pills?" she muttered.
The head said "YOU'RE EXPELLED!"

Then I told him what a mess
Miss looked in that dress.
"An' you in your grey and blue
Look like 1962!"

It just ain't fair! Nothin's fair!
It isn't fair! It's not!
They don't care if I'm not there!
An' I don't care! SO WHAT!

Marvellous Martin

Oh, Martin! You're so marvellous!
Your face is really fabulous!
Even your feet are glamorous!
We love you! You know we do!

Oh, Martin! You're so beautiful!
The way you walk is wonderful!
Your voice is just incredible!
Gold doesn't shine like you!

Oh, Martin! You are gorgeous!
Your muscles are enormous!
Your skin is really glorious!
You look so sparkly and new!

Oh, Martin! We're in love with you!
We just can't get enough of you!
Your hair waves like a double-U!
Your eyes are the deepest blue!

Oh, Martin won't go out with us,
Won't disco-dance and shout with us,
No, he won't hang about with us,
'COS HE LOVES MARTIN, TOO!

Nicker Nick

"Who took the rubber off my desk?

Who took my ruler and my pencils?

Who took my felts and didn't ask?

And who's got my Tom and Jerry stencils?"

"It was Nick, Bess,

Nick.

Nicker Nick.

He crept up sly and slick, Bess.

Then ran away real quick!"

"Who's got a lunch-box same as mine?

The red one. You know. Liverpool Football
                                                    Club.

Well look! They've left theirs here with
                                                    nothing in!

And taken mine and all my lovely grub!"

"It was Nick, Ed,

Nick.

Nicker Nick.

He did the same to Rick, Ed.

And now he's being sick!"

"Who said my mum was here for me?

Waiting in the office with the nurse?

Well, I went down there, didn't I, to see.

And now they've whipped the money from
                                                    my purse!"

"It was Nick, Chris,

Nick.

Nicker Nick.

That's his favourite trick, Chris.

He must think we're all thick!"

"Who's got my things! Who robbed my tray!

Who took my bike? My bag? Oh, please!

Who's got my coat? Who was it, hey?

Oh, Miss! Oh, I've been burgled! Call the police!"

"It was us, Nick,

Us!

Me and all the class!

But don't make such a fuss, Nick.

You won't need yours AND ours!"

Oinky Ollie

"I'm starving! I'm famished!
Who's got grub to spare?
Oh, great! Banana sandwich!
Oh, yes! A squashy pear!"

"Just take it! Take it Ollie!
We're all feeling ill.
This coach is really smelly
And it swerves around as well."

"I'm ravenous! I'm hollow!
Coo! Cheers! Cold Christmas pud!
Oh, ham! All fatty and yellow!
And beef all red with blood!"

"Have it! Keep it, Ollie!
Take it right away.
I've got a gurgly belly
And I'm feeling sort of grey."

"I'm empty! Really hungry!
Let's have those garlic dips!
And that curried cod with chutney.
I love cold fish and chips!"

"Look! Ollie's gone all quiet!
Hey, Ol! You feeling worse?
Oh, look! The sick-bag diet!
His stomach's in reverse!"

Poorly Paulie

Dear Miss Quilter,

    I really am so sorry.

    Poor Paul has got his throat again.

    It's such an awful worry.

    Yesterday he felt so weak.

    On Tuesday he was hot.

    On Monday he was nearly sick.

    Last week he had a spot.

    His little eyes are full of cold.

    His ears! Poor little chap!

    Thank goodness that he's not too old

    For snuggles on my lap.

    There's TONSILLITIS on his toe

    And TOOTHACHE on his bottom.

    His old MALARIA just won't go.

    And all these new things – HE'S GOT 'EM!

I'd send him back right now. This term.

But oh! What rows and dramas

About your new school uniform!

Oh, couldn't he wear pyjamas?

He'd feel so cosy, then, and warm.

And could he bring his teddy?

And maybe, somewhere in your room,

You could fit his little beddy.

Dear Mrs Hunter,

WHO IS PAUL?

We really can't remember.

Is he the lad who came to school

For an hour in September?

Why don't you keep him safe indoors?

Play surgeons. Get the message?

Stitch up the little blighter's jaws!

Use Black and Decker massage!

Inject him with a BAYONET!

Use sledge-hammer anaesthetic.

Make scalpel marks around HIS THROAT!

Give him cyanide tonic!

Tie his neck in a hangman's sling!

BE BRAVE! BE BOLD! BE CRUEL!

Try bullet pills! Or anything!

BUT DON'T SEND HIM TO SCHOOL!

Quarrelsome Quentin

"Oh Quentin! You're in!
Come on! We're gonna win!
You can play
Up front today.
You're bound to score again!"

      "Not football! What plonkers!
      Footie's really bonkers!
      You rush about
      And get puffed out.
      Let's go and get some conkers."

"Oh! Great idea!
There's loads of 'em this year.
Come on! Let's go
And get 'em now
Before they disappear."

"Not me! Oh no!
I'm not coming. So!
I've had enough
Of conkers and stuff.
Let's play 'Dare and Go'!"

"Oh yeah! Oh yeah!
Let's have a game of 'Dare'!
You and Demster
Release the hamster
And leave this fur glove there!"

"Oh, we'll be dead!
You must be off your head!
We'll all be caught
And on report!
LET'S PLAY FOOTIE INSTEAD!"

Romantic Rosie

"Give us a kiss for Christmas!
It's gotta be on the lips!"
She grabs you like an octopus
And slobbers till it drips.
"I've got mistletoe!" she'll cry.
MISTLETOE! IN JULY!

Last week in Country Dancing
She just ignored the teachers.
Instead of "Cumberland Reel"
SHE was doing smooches!
Not stars and tapping feet –
But slow ones! Cheek to cheek!

Yesterday in Science
Miss said "We're thinking about bones."
Rosie got Jack and held his hand
And wouldn't let it go.
"Your fingers are lovely," she said.
And poor old Jack went red.

Guess why I'm in a hurry
To get out of school today.
And why I'll be ill tomorrow
And have to be away.
Well, I've just found this note in my shoe.
'I love you,' it says. 'From Guess Who?'

Scarer Sarah

"BOO!
YAHOO!
I'm gonna getcha! WOO!
I'm the ghost
Of Big Bad Boast!
I'm gonna getcha! BOO!"

Scarer Sarah
Runs round and round,
Scaring all the lit-luns
In the lit-luns' playground.

"WAH!
YA-HA!
I'm gonna killya! BAH!
I'm the spirit
Of Ghostly Garrett!
I'm gonna killya! WAH!"

Scarer Sarah
Runs up and down,
Scaring all the big kids
In the big kids' playground.

"POW!
YE-OW!
I'm gonna catchya! WOW!
I'm the spectre
Of Headless Hector!
I'm gonna catchya! POW!"

Scarer Sarah
Runs from her tomb,
Scaring all the teachers
In the teachers' staffroom!

Tell-Tale Tara

"Ian's gone to prison
Because he swore at Miss.
And Rosie's getting married.
You have to if you kiss.

They're closing down the school.
I saw it on the telly.
'Cos the teachers shout so much
And the loos are always smelly.

There's a monster in the playground!
It eats you up at play!
It's gobbled loads of lit-luns!
That's why they're all away.

Edward Thompson's mother
Was told off by the police
'Cos she packs him horrid sandwiches
With wholemeal bread and cheese!

I'm going to be famous!
Don't tell, 'cos no-one knows.
I'm gonna be in *Neighbours*!
And I'm having a new nose."

"Tara Smith's the greatest,
The biggest you have come across.
The fastest, the most famous
LIAR in the Universe!"

Upper-Class Ursula

Keep away! Don't touch!
I'm rather special, you know.
Mother is half Dutch.
Father owns Saville Row.
Home is an awfully super detached,
Terribly grand and just so.

I'm superior. I'm great.
I'm related to the Queen.
She's actually really rather sweet,
Quite charming on the phone.
I may be queen myself next week,
She said I could have a go.

Don't stare so. Don't smile.
You're all so dreadfully low.
I'm moving to a posher school
Where girls with breeding go.
Girls who walk in single file,
Saying "DAR-LING" and "HELL-O".

Oh, sweetie, don't jaw.
It's awfully common to row.
You really can be such a bore.
Do stop that screaming, now.
Oh, please don't scrab me any more.
GET OFF, YOU FLIPPIN' COW!

Vulgar Vicky

Vulgar Vicky picks her nose,
Peels off scabs and sucks her toes,
Dribbles custard, makes it run
And scribbles things inside *The Sun*.

Vulgar Vicky swears like mad
And talks about sex and things real bad,
Shows her knickers, breathes bad air
And shakes the dandruff from her hair.

The Lady Mayor arrived at school.
Vicky said "Welcome, Most Wonderful.
You must be hungry, Your Worship-ness.
Have some jelly. I sneezed you this!

I've picked you something fresh, home-grown.
My newest spot. It's 'Pick-Your-Own'!
There's ear-wax honey, nice and thick,
And armpit garlic – like a lick?"

The Lady Mayor smiled her smile,
Raised her skirt and turned with style,
Bent down double, showed her rump
And trumped a glorious, gaseous TRUMP!

"My de-ah," she said, yanking off her shoes.
"Try these tasty, toe-nail chews!
And here's a bogey lolly for ya!
My name, my sweet, is LADY VICTORIA!"

Whee-ee Willy

Whee-ee!

Whee-ee!

I'm an eagle! I'm free-ee!

I'll get you!

I'll gut you!

I'll grate you with chee-eese!

I'll munch you!

I'll crunch you

For lunch and for tea-ea!

Whee-ee!

Whee-ee!

I'm a jet Cherokee-ee!

I bomb!

And I boom!

And I brr-rr-rrm through the tree-ees!

I stalk!

And I stoop!

And I sting like a bee-ee!

Whee-ee!

Whee-ee!

I'm Dracula, see-ee!

I shriek!

And I seek!

And I suck arterie-ies!

I sip a blood-cola!

I slurp a blood-soda!

I drink you!

I drain you!

Then go for a wee-ee!

Xylophone Xenia

Xenia! Xenia!

She's like a skeleton

But skinnier!

We use her bones

For xylophones

And play her in the orchestra!

We THUMP her thumbs

On kettle drums!

We KNOCK her knees on barrels!

We TAP her limbs

For gentle hymns

And SMASH them hard for carols!

We TWANG her tongue!

We RUB her ribs!

We TINKLE on her tibia!

We RUMBLE-PLAY

Her vertebrae!

And FIDDLE on her fibula!

We SCRAPE her jaws

With tenon saws –

The Head has tried to ban them –

And BASH her skull

To help the school

To sing THE NATIONAL ANTHEM!

Yelling Yasmin

"Oh, stop the assembly, Miss Quilter!
There's guns going off! Hear that crack?
Into the air-raid shelter!
The school is under attack!"

"Oh, Yasmin, please stop shivering.
Don't panic. Get down from the wall.
It's only a lorry delivering.
It's only the man with the oil."

"The school's falling over! It's tumbling!
Get everyone out of the gate!
Oh look! Can't you see, Miss? It's toppling!
Get running before it's too late!"

"Oh, Yasmin, please don't cry, dear.
There's no need to make such a fuss.
It's only the clouds racing by, dear.
You don't need to run for the bus."

"There's water all round us! It's rising!
We're sinking! Find something that floats!
Send a flare up! The school is capsizing!
Non-swimmers get into the boats!"

"Oh, Yasmin, it's only a puddle.
Poor Jack has made a small mess.
We don't need canoes or a paddle.
Now, Yasmin, get yourself dressed."

"I'm dying! I've got this pneumonia!
My tummy! My throat, Miss! My head!
Oh, please get my mummy! Oh, phone her!
I'll have to go home to my bed!"

"Yes, Yasmin, you're right. You look bad, dear!
Oh scream, dear! And stamp, dear! And cry!
Oh yell! That's the way! You go mad, dear!
Yes, run out of school, dear! GOODBYE!"

Zzzz Zoe

"Er, Zoe. Are you quite awake?"

"Oh yes, I was listening, Miss."

"Then, what do blue and yellow make?"

"Oh the sea, rippling dreamily, Miss."

"Oh Zoe! You really are hopeless!

You're always half asleep!

Yawning! And dopey! And helpless!

Sit up now! Sit up on your seat!

Now, everyone. Use lots of TEXTURE.

Put masses of TONE in your work."

"Er. Please Miss. What is the picture?"

"A sunset! A sunset! You twerp!"

A sunset . . . All peaceful . . . And cosy . . .
Warm evening . . . Warm colours . . . Warm bed . . .
Everything pinkish . . . And rosy . . .
I think . . . I'll just lay down . . . my head . . .

"Oh Zoe! Get up off the pallet!
Get up child! You're dozing again!
Your cheeks are all purple and violet!
There's a great golden sun on your chin!"

"Oh, I wasn't asleep, Miss, or fainting.
I was trying some FACE ART. Alright?
I'm doing an Aztec mask painting.
I must do some more, now. Goodnight."

ATTENDANCE REGISTER

CLASS TEACHER Miss M. Quilter

REGISTRATION NUMBER	NAME	M 12	T 13	W 14	T 15	F 16	M 19	T 20	W 21
			JUNE						
1	Amazing Amelia	/\	/\	/\					
2	Bossy Bessy	/\	/\	/\					
3	Creepy Chrissy	/\	/\	/\					
4	Dangerous Danny	/\	\	/\					
5	Exploding Ed	/O	/\	/O					
6	Flashy Floyd	/\	/\	/\					
7	Graffiti Greg	/\	/\	/\					
8	Hurricane Harry	/\	/\	\					
9	Insulting Ian	/\	/\	/\					
10	J-Jumpy J-Jack	OO	/\	/\					
11	Ketchup Kelly	/\	/\	/\					
12	Lipstick Lizzie	/\	OO	OO					
13	Marvellous Martin	/\	/\	/\					
14	Nicker Nick	O\	O\	O\					
15	Oinky Ollie	/\	OO	/\					
16	Poorly Paulie	OO	OO	OO					
17	Quarrelsome Quentin	/\	/\	/\					
18	Romantic Rosie	/\	/\	/\					
19	Scarer Sarah	/\	/\	/\					
20	Tell-Tale Tara	/\	/\	/\					
21	Upper-Class Ursula	OO	/\	/\					
22	Vulgar Vicky	/\	/\	/\					
23	Whee-ee Willy	/\	/\	/\					
24	Xylophone Xenia	/\	/\	/\					
25	Yelling Yasmin	/\	/\	/\					
26	Zzzz Zoe	L\	L\	L\					
27									